ENGAGING MINDS
IN Social Studies Classrooms

Engaging Minds in the Classroom: The Surprising Power of Joy
by Michael F. Opitz and Michael P. Ford

Engaging Minds in English Language Arts Classrooms: The Surprising Power of Joy
by Mary Jo Fresch
edited by Michael F. Opitz and Michael P. Ford

Engaging Minds in Science and Math Classrooms: The Surprising Power of Joy
by Eric Brunsell and Michelle A. Fleming
edited by Michael F. Opitz and Michael P. Ford

ENGAGING MINDS
IN Social Studies Classrooms

THE SURPRISING POWER OF **JOY**

JAMES A. EREKSON

Edited by
Michael F. Opitz & Michael P. Ford

ASCD

Alexandria, Virginia USA

1703 N. Beauregard St. • Alexandria, VA 22311-1714 USA
Phone: 800-933-2723 or 703-578-9600 • Fax: 703-575-5400
Website: www.ascd.org • E-mail: member@ascd.org
Author guidelines: www.ascd.org/write

Gene R. Carter, *Executive Director;* Richard Papale, *Interim Chief Program Development Officer;* Stefani Roth, *Interim Publisher;* Laura Lawson and Stefani Roth, *Acquisitions Editors;* Allison Scott, *Development Editor;* Julie Houtz, *Director, Book Editing & Production;* Darcie Russell, *Senior Associate Editor;* Georgia Park, *Senior Graphic Designer;* Mike Kalyan, *Production Manager;* Barton Matheson Willse & Worthington, *Typesetter;* Andrea Wilson, *Production Specialist*

Printed in the United States of America. Cover art © 2014 ASCD. ASCD publications present a variety of viewpoints. The views expressed or implied in this book should not be interpreted as official positions of the Association. All referenced trademarks are the property of their respective owners.

All web links in this book are correct as of the publication date below but may have become inactive or otherwise modified since that time. If you notice a deactivated or changed link, please e-mail books@ascd.org with the words "Link Update" in the subject line. In your message, please specify the web link, the book title, and the page number on which the link appears.

PAPERBACK ISBN: 978-1-4166-1727-3   ASCD product #113022   n2/14
Also available as an e-book (see *Books in Print* for the ISBNs).

Quantity discounts: 10–49 copies, 10%; 50+ copies, 15%; for 1,000 or more copies, call 800-933-2723, ext. 5634, or 703-575-5634. For desk copies: www.ascd.org/deskcopy

Library of Congress Cataloging-in-Publication Data

Erekson, James A.
    Engaging minds in social studies classrooms : the surprising power of joy / James A. Erekson ; Michael F. Opitz and Michael P. Ford, eds.
        pages cm.
    Includes bibliographical references and index.
        ISBN 978-1-4166-1727-3 (pbk. : alk. paper)
1. Social sciences—Study and teaching. 2. Social science teachers—Training of. 3. Motivation in education. 4. Effective teaching. I. Opitz, Michael F., editor. II. Ford, Michael P., editor. III. Title.
    LB1584.E48 2014
    372.83—dc23
                                                                                    2013046271

23 22 21 20 19 18 17 16 15 14   1 2 3 4 5 6 7 8 9 10 11 12

ENGAGING MINDS
in Social Studies Classrooms

THE SURPRISING POWER OF **JOY**

Acknowledgments. vii

Introduction 1

1. Understanding Joyful Learning in Social Studies 5

2. Evaluating and Assessing Joyful Learning 13

3. Implementing Joyful Learning in Social Studies. 23

4. Using Joyful Learning to Support Education Initiatives. 43

References 50

Index. 54

About the Author 57

About the Editors 58

Acknowledgments

Many thanks to Mark Lee High, whose master teaching in both social studies and literacy is an ongoing inspiration to me, and who provided me with invaluable opportunities to work alongside him and his students in Gunnison, Colorado. Special thanks are due to Lindsey Moses, Arizona State University, for providing me with vital tips for teachers of English language learners. I also express gratitude to Mike Opitz and Mike Ford (Mike[2], as we came to call them), who are not only excellent editors but also powerful mentors. The book was a joy to write, with all these wonderful people to work with.

Introduction

It seems to me that most students are not born with intrinsic motivation for social studies; methods of attending closely to abstract structures and evidence must be taught, modeled, and applied. When I talk to people who love history, for example, they will often reference a specific class and teacher who helped to "wake them up" to history—which suggests, unfortunately, that up until that point other teachers had put them to sleep.

A joyful approach to teaching social studies embraces the fact that student motivation and engagement are at the top of the curriculum. Therefore, when planning social studies lessons, teachers need to address these affective aspects of learning, to be able to assess and discuss both cognitive and noncognitive outcomes as aspects of student growth.

Considering Noncognitive Skills

Research in neuroscience has taught us that there are connections between the deep, old areas of the brain (the hippocampus and amygdala) that house our sense of fear, safety, risk, and enjoyment and the newer surface areas of the brain that control our problem solving, rational thought, and planning (Medina, 2008). The "thinking" areas of the brain are inextricably wired to the "feeling" areas of the brain; that is, cognitive memory is connected to affective experience. The implication is that if educators hope to achieve powerful learning, they must enlist learners' minds and hearts simultaneously. The joyful learning framework offers an opportunity to do just that.

Overview

In *Engaging Minds in the Classroom: The Surprising Power of Joy* (2014), Michael Opitz and Michael Ford present a framework for joyful teaching and learning that can be implemented in all content areas. The framework comprises motivational generalizations, factors to assess and evaluate when creating a joyful learning environment, and areas in which to promote learning. In this book, I discuss how to implement the joyful learning framework in the social studies classroom.

In Chapter 1, I outline foundational definitions and explain how joyful learning applies to social studies, providing information teachers can use to up the ante on engagement and motivation and stimulate student interest in all areas of social studies. This information also can help teachers frame discussions about joyful learning as needed in professional development situations, including discussions with other teachers and administrators.

Educators who want to enable joyful learning need an organized vision for how they and their students spend time in school. So, in Chapter 2, I discuss five elements that must be assessed in any effort to promote joyful learning in social studies:

- Learners,
- Teachers,
- Texts and materials,
- Assessments, and
- Schoolwide configurations.

Chapter 3 is the bread-and-butter chapter, with suggestions on what to do and how to do it. I provide some practical suggestions for implementing joyful learning in social studies classrooms; each suggestion aligns with principles of joyful learning as outlined in Chapter 1 and the elements discussed in Chapter 2, and prioritizes student engagement and motivation. Chapter 3 is intended to support teachers in applying the principles of joyful learning in planning specific classroom activities—while understanding why they are doing what they are doing.

In Chapter 4, I discuss some of the contemporary demands educators face, especially policy demands that can make teachers feel less than joyful about prospects for learners, including:

- Response to Intervention,
- Achievement gaps and the need to accelerate student achievement,
- The Common Core State Standards and national social studies standards, and
- Accountability and assessment.

Connecting with diverse learners, particularly English language learners (ELLs), is a focus of the *Engaging Minds* series; throughout this book, you'll find teaching tips that suggest specific strategies and highlight research on how to support ELLs in social studies.

Conclusion

I believe that teachers can provide joyful social studies learning experiences while actively responding to contemporary demands. However, sometimes the optimism and emotion involved in the topic of joyful learning is seen as fluff and frill. Despite the common sense of joyful learning, despite research findings that clearly integrate joyful learning with cognitive academic outcomes, some continue to be skeptical of an approach to learning and learners that involves what they perceive as the "touchy-feely" aspects of human thinking. Ignoring these affective aspects of learners and learning, however, is ultimately detrimental to the learning process. Indeed, one might even attribute many of the educational failures of the past 60 years to a myopic focus on cognitive and behavioral learning and the rational and empirical aspects of content (Ravitch, 2010).

More recently, researchers have begun to return to noncognitive aspects of academic growth. A team from the University of Chicago published a monograph correlating noncognitive aspects of education with academic outcomes (Farrington et al., 2012). One correlation is between mindset and performance (see Dweck, 2006): An academic mindset includes a sense of belonging, belief in one's effort, belief that one can succeed, and value of the work. Each of these aspects is more related to research on motivation and engagement than it is to cognitive processes such as information processing—and each is a component of joyful learning.

Opitz and Ford's (2014) definition of *joy* encompasses more than simple fun or entertainment. As I discuss in Chapter 1, learners will experience more enjoyment, feel more involved, and buy into their educational experiences when their schoolwork is oriented to joyful learning. Fun and entertainment may be products of joyful learning, but they are not the goal.

I join the other authors and editors of these books on engaging minds in adopting a broad view of joyful learning, reaching through research and scientific inquiry into philosophy. Our most powerful and involved moments with learners are always punctuated by a kind of joy, whether this stems from feelings connected to competence in asking questions, from interest in the content, or from students forging an identity based on the kind of learning they do in our classrooms. In order to create effective lesson and unit plans, to use accurate assessment instruments, and to present content effectively, we need to incorporate what is known about the noncognitive aspects of learning. My purpose in writing this book is to show social studies teachers how to organize and structure the work of joyful learning to benefit their students; my goal is for powerful and involved learning moments to feel less like a matter of luck and more like a matter of purpose and design.

CHAPTER 1

Understanding Joyful Learning in Social Studies

Joyful teaching and learning in social studies encompasses "acquiring knowledge or skills in ways that cause pleasure and happiness" (Opitz & Ford, 2014, p. 10). As discussed in the Introduction, the joyful learning process requires and builds on noncognitive skills as well as academic knowledge. Skills such as resilience, persistence, determination, and a willingness to problem solve lay the foundation for joy in learning. Structuring teaching practice around affective outcomes capitalizes on the pleasures of learning and leads to knowledge, thinking, and inquiry.

The National Council for the Social Studies (2010) has described the goal of social studies as "the promotion of civic competence—the knowledge, intellectual processes, and democratic dispositions required of students to be *active and engaged participants in public life*" [emphasis added] (p. 210). Therefore, success in the learning process for social studies learners results in effective participation in public life. Teachers can support this goal if they are able to help students develop knowledge, thinking processes, and an inquiring disposition.

Learning and development is encouraged by different types of rewards: autonomous, social, and tension/release (Olson, 2009). Specific examples of these rewards are the innate pleasure of a learning experience, feedback and encouragement, and the pleasure that comes from overcoming a potential stressful situation to achieve. Focusing on joyful learning ensures that these types of reward outcomes for students are incorporated in activities in the social studies classroom.

Joyful teaching and learning in social studies depend on sustainable long-term inquiry—across a whole school year or longer—that helps students see the big picture. Planning a single day's lesson or a two-week unit needs to be part of a much larger vision. This vision includes not only the content objectives of the curriculum but also the participation of and interaction with the learner. When striving to create a joyful learning environment, it is important to understand how essential students' motivation and engagement will be to its success.

Motivation and Engagement

Although many people use the words *engagement* and *motivation* as if they were synonymous, differences in connotation are important for our practice as teachers. *Motivation* is the drive or the cause of actions. *Engagement* describes how people think and act while they are in the thick of the action. Motivation creates a narrative arc for what people do, framing it with a beginning and a projected ending. But as with most good stories, the meat of the narrative happens in the middle, under the arc. Focusing on student motivation generates outcomes in engagement. When students are engaged learners, joy emanates from success in the learning process (Rantala & Maatta, 2012; Schlechty, 2011; Tough, 2012).

In their foundational book for this series, Opitz and Ford (2014) outlined factors that influence motivation, including self-efficacy and competence beliefs, attributions and control beliefs, perceptions of value, and goal orientation. Figure 1.1 illustrates how we can use understanding of these motivational factors to enhance our teaching of social studies.

Any discussion of motivation and engagement must address the concept of entertainment and audience (i.e., student) participation. The key difference between entertainment and education is direction: whereas entertainment is directed toward an audience, education is the effort to draw the audience out—eliciting interaction. Entertainment expects little effort on the

FIGURE 1.1
Generalizations About Motivation, and Implications for the Social Studies Classroom

Generalization	Definition	Instructional Implications
Adaptive self-efficacy and competence beliefs motivate students.	Students judge their identity with reference to general tasks ("I'm good at writing," or "I do well in history") and also project how well they expect to perform ("I can find evidence for this question").	• Help students identify moments when they display knowledge, thinking processes, and democratic dispositions by specifically labeling these: "You are good at comparing and contrasting"; "You remembered the facts that mattered the most"; "You could tell how that rule was fair and unfair." • Be honest about challenges and expectations. The more specific the task, the more likely teachers are able to be optimistic about telling students what they already know how to do.
Adaptive attributions and control beliefs motivate students.	Students ascribe success and failure to factors either inside or outside the individual (quality of studying vs. the quality of a teacher's lecture) and the degree of control the individual has (e.g., luck vs. effort).	• Cause and effect is a common theme in social studies. • Use inquiry questions about successes and failures to help students gain a frame of reference for how the logic of attribution works. • Specifically address attribution of control and how it leads to broader consequences in society.
Higher levels of value motivate students.	Students believe that investment of time and effort makes them good people within cultural spheres.	Extend social studies to the world outside the school; illustrate for students how content applies to the broader world of public life.
Goals motivate and direct students.	*Goal content* focuses on establishing something to attain, and *goal orientation* focuses on the purpose or reason for engaging in an activity. *Mastery goal orientation* encourages students to approach a task in order to learn it well and gain new competence. *Performance goal orientation* leads one to demonstrate ability for others to seek reward or recognition (Rueda, 2011).	Look for ways to balance different kinds of goals. • Specific content objectives may lack a broader sense of purpose, and thus need to be balanced. • Focus on performance and social competence may overshadow the intrinsic value of mastery. • Create assessments that put various types of goals in balance or allow students flexibility to set their own goals.

Generalizations adapted from Pintrich, Marx, & Boyle (1993); table adapted from Opitz & Ford (2014, p. 12–13).

part of the audience; any engagement stems almost entirely from the qualities and design of the presentation. Engagement in education venues should rely less on the external "entertaining" qualities of presentation (although these are part of the social studies teacher's toolkit) and more on the student's internalized attributes of inquiry and the satisfaction experienced in pursuing evidence.

Students will encounter multiple presentations of information along the way, and they will certainly need to be able to evaluate how well these presentations are crafted. However, very little powerful growth in social studies happens under a transmission model of learning and teaching. Student research and inquiry, service learning, and performance outcomes are better suited to an active, student-oriented model of concept development in social studies. Rather than putting on a show, teachers should orchestrate progress for many students addressing different aspects of projects.

My suggestion of incorporating students into projects does not to discourage teachers from presenting material in a dramatic way. Doing something a little out of the ordinary such as wearing period costumes can make historical images concrete for learners, while also modeling our own love for and identification with social studies. Incorporating this kind of showmanship only a few times a year makes entertainment a kind of punctuation on the broader paragraphs and pages of students' ongoing inquiry.

Motivating and Engaging Students in Social Studies

Success in social studies depends on learners building new concepts, making connections to their lives, and overcoming misconceptions (Brophy & Alleman, 2007). At the same time, social studies makes powerful demands on vocabulary learning. Any kind of concept development takes time, and we should encourage our students to ask the type of social studies questions that further conceptual growth:

- Why do people do what they do?
- Who makes the decisions?
- Who is in charge and how did they get there? Who is following, and why?

- Who wants what, and what is the result of these desires?
- What changes as years pass?

Units of study in social studies should be broad enough to allow students to consider these questions over months of time; they are not linked to any specific unit, but rather provide a foundation for learning. A broad approach to social studies may mean teaching fewer topics per year, but it will result in greater depth and conceptual development.

Students need time to process information. Too often we prepare information and teach it as if the students had been there with us while we prepared. When we present new information, we have to remember that students need time to connect and think about it. There are many variations on the theme of asking and answering questions; using strategies such as pair-share give students an opportunity to take new information and *do something with it right now*.

> Time to process information is particularly important for ELLs. Remember, many students are processing what you are presenting and also attempting to translate it into their first language. They need time to process, discuss, and clarify.

Student Choice and Autonomy

The best way to incorporate choice and autonomy in social studies assignments is to offer students a menu of options; I have found that it is easier for students to select than to identify their own ideas for inquiry. However, we should give our strongest students the opportunity to think and choose freely, or we will miss an opportunity to help them grow. Remember, all the growth we encourage in social studies classes is supposed to lead to active, engaged participation in public life—now, not sometime later in life. Providing students choices in how to demonstrate their understanding engages them and encourages this active participation.

> Although teachers need to offer inquiry opportunities appropriate for their ELL students' content and language proficiency, eliminating choice is not always the best option. Choice and background knowledge on topics of interest facilitate vocabulary development and comprehension.

We also should offer students some measure of choice in working independently or collaboratively. In middle school classes, there are always one or two students who just cannot stop talking and are often moving around the classroom and interrupting other students. Looking at this as a student need rather than a distraction, however, can change our approach to teaching social studies. Offering these "social butterflies" the opportunity to work with others helps them succeed as learners. Similarly, other students prefer to work alone, and we need to include those opportunities as well. This is consistent with social developmental theory (Vygotsky, 1978); whereas some need public dialogue to structure their learning and thinking, others prefer to engage in private silent dialogue. Teachers who are in tune with students' social preferences and needs as learners can design flexible groupings (Opitz, 1998) that follow students' ideas for what they want and need in social studies.

Self-Assessment

In all areas of sociology and psychology, researchers worry about the biasing effects of self-reported data—that people are likely to say what they think they *should* say instead of what they really think or feel. However, when compared with objective measures of happiness such as having needs met, having opportunities for fulfillment, or having degrees of freedom in life, self-reports match tidily (Diener, 2000; Stone, Schwartz, Broderick, & Deaton, 2010).

What this means for us as teachers is that we can gather useful information about joyful teaching and learning by talking with students. We also need to share information about their subjective well-being. As we discover and experience joy and challenges in our own social studies inquiries, thinking aloud about these experiences models self-assessment and helps students feel enabled to communicate in school about their own experience.

The same principle of self-reporting can be used in structured assessments to gather information on students' interests, attitudes, and identities. Opitz, Ford, and Erekson (2011) presented inventories, surveys, and interview protocols as structures for self-reporting data. One reason for collecting structured data of this type is that when they are compiled for an entire class, teachers can analyze them for trends and patterns that influence teaching decisions (e.g., to structure inquiry learning activities). Anecdotal notes taken during learner conferences will provide valuable additional data to triangulate what is learned using more structured instruments.

Student attitudes toward social studies depend on them having a schema of social studies, which they acquire only through participation over time. Interviews and discussions where students can define social studies may be as important as asking how they feel about the time blocks with that subject name. In their classic study, Stodolsky, Salk, and Glaessner (1991) found that elementary students' concepts of social studies lack unifying themes and consensus; it is an abstract label that students have a hard time grasping. It is difficult for students to identify with a subject that is ill defined; they are more likely to identify with specific, narrow areas of content they already know (Stodolsky et al., 1991, p. 98). Thus asking them how much they like it makes less sense than getting them to discuss what it is, and then following up with questions evaluating attitude.

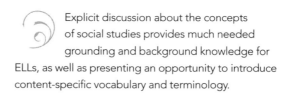 Explicit discussion about the concepts of social studies provides much needed grounding and background knowledge for ELLs, as well as presenting an opportunity to introduce content-specific vocabulary and terminology.

A Framework for Joyful Learning

Ward and Dahlmeier (2011) noted that "as a teaching and learning goal, [joy] is . . . an optimal experience that occurs when someone is making positive choices, is in control of his or her own actions, and is making connections" (p. 94). As Wolk (2008) observed, we need to nurture students' pursuit of joy of learning. Opitz and Ford's (2014) joyful learning framework provides a structure for ensuring students this optimal experience. The framework (see Figure 1.2) consists of three parts:

1. **Five motivational generalizations**: adaptive self-efficacy and competence beliefs, adaptive attributions and beliefs about control, higher levels of interest and intrinsic motivation, higher levels of value, and goals.

2. **Five elements that need to be assessed** and evaluated in order to get the most from joyful learning: learners, teachers, texts and materials, assessments, and schoolwide configurations.

3. **Five key areas** in which to promote joyful learning: school community, physical environment, whole-group instruction, small-group instruction, and individual instruction.

The joyful learning framework is effective in helping students succeed and become lifelong learners because it capitalizes on what we know about how to best motivate students, enables us to build on what we currently know about engagement, and focuses on the whole child. The "whole child" is intellectually active; creative and curious; empathetic, kind, caring, and fair; and a critical thinker, among other attributes (ASCD, 2007).

The goal of this book is to empower teachers to create an environment in which students experience joyful learning. In the next chapter, I discuss how to assess how well the five elements of your environmental setting contribute to joyful learning.

FIGURE 1.2
Joyful Learning Framework

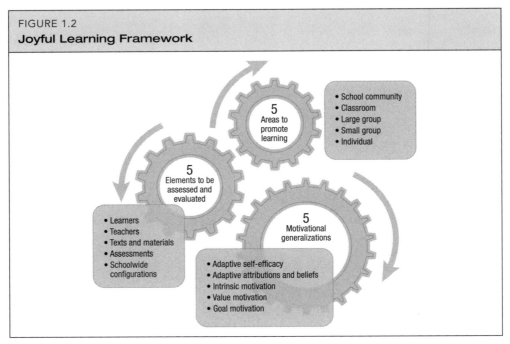

Source: Reprinted from Opitz and Ford (2014, p. 14)

CHAPTER 2

Evaluating and Assessing Joyful Learning

Just as there are many beliefs, values, and structures that underpin successful teaching, there are also different elements within the classroom environment that influence learning. These elements must be addressed to sustain joyful teaching and learning. As part of the process of establishing a joyful learning environment, we must evaluate not only the learners themselves, but ourselves as teachers; the texts, materials, and assessments we use; and schoolwide configurations.

Evaluating Learners

Students' beliefs about their own competence and identity influence their willingness to try, and thus their ability to engage. However, assessing and evaluating the affective outcomes that contribute to joyful learning can be complicated, because affective outcomes such as motivation are multifaceted and complex and not easily defined (Guthrie & Wigfield, 1997). As Opitz and Ford (2014) noted, engagement often results from a combination of expecting success (*self-efficacy*), seeing the outcome as important, and feeling safe in the learning environment. Our assessment of learners, then, should be guided by three overarching questions:

- Do learners think they can succeed?
- Do learners want to succeed?
- Do learners know what they need to do to succeed?

These questions provide the basis for student inventories or surveys that should be implemented before instruction begins (see Figure 2.1). Spending time conducting informal assessments starting on the first day of school will actually make it easier to design year-long learning settings and to set long-term goals. Consider the value in the early days of school of presenting students with sample issues, problems, and materials. Give yourself an opportunity to watch, take notes, and ask students questions; take time to learn about your learners. Teachers cannot skimp on knowing about students. We reap what we sow, and if our earliest efforts are to understand our students as learners, we will reap rewards throughout the rest of the school year.

Consider the influence of language acquisition on learners' identity, self-efficacy, and anxiety. In addition to the content, do your ELLs think they can be successful with the language used in social studies?

Evaluating Ourselves as Teachers

Like many other service careers, teaching is defined as a "helping relationship." Mark Wasicsko (2007) focused on discovering how effective teachers view their relationships with people, and he was able to identify some common traits. Effective teachers anticipate that other teachers are capable, identify and connect with other teachers, and believe that all teachers have a larger sense of purpose. Effective teachers' understanding of others and their own goals both extend beyond the immediate to larger implication and contexts.

Despite the persistence of research findings indicating that the individual teacher is what makes the most difference to learners (Wright, Horn, & Sanders, 1997), many people in our society seem to think effective teachers are naturally gifted or that effective teaching happens by accident (Hattie, 2012). Not so! Great teachers do not appear by magic: we grow as we work, and we learn on the job. Evaluating ourselves as both teacher and learner should be part of our long-term commitment to professional development. This evaluation must delve into our own perceptions and biases; what we as teachers think and believe about learners can make a difference in making our teaching experiences joyful.

FIGURE 2.1 Evaluating Learners in Social Studies	
Identity	How do students identify with questions and issues about social interaction? How do students identify with participation in public life?
Self-efficacy	Do my students believe they can be successful at asking social science and humanities questions? Do my students believe they can be successful participants in public life?
Anxiety	Do my students suffer from anxieties or misconceptions that make them feel at risk when asking their questions? Do their anxieties or fears prevent them from participating in public life?
Curiosity and interest	Do my students show curiosity about how social interactions work, or about how to participate in the public sphere? Do my students show interest in topics and ideas from the social sciences and humanities? When given choices, what topics and ideas appeal to my students?
Value	Do my students place importance on understanding social studies content? Do my students see connections between social studies and their lives? Do my students think learning in social studies is worth the investment of time and effort?
Perception of challenge	How do my students compare perceptions of their own skill to the perceived demands of the content?
Goal orientation	Do my students tend to set goals to grow in understanding or to complete performances? How do my students react to failure?
Self-regulating behaviors	How do my students reflect on their own learning? Are students able to talk about their own growth and development in social studies?
Persistence	Do my students persevere when faced with a challenging learning task?
Prosocial behaviors	How do my students participate in a community of learners, especially when faced with challenging work?

What Is My Identity as a Learner?

In evaluating your own effect as a teacher on students' identities as learn-ers, consider how your identity *as a learner* affects your teaching. As teachers we are learners; the questions that we ask about our students' engagement and motivation provide a basis for us to reflect on our own

FIGURE 2.2	
Evaluating Ourselves as Teachers: Identity Statements	
I am engaged in learning.	I am always looking for what is most effective and most active. I try to change not only myself but my environment. I want feedback. I talk more with people than at them. Challenges engage me. I set high expectations for myself and others. I learn well when I have the chance to notice mistakes. The language of social studies belongs to me.
I use ongoing self-evaluation to help plan my teaching and learning.	My great successes are strong questions that lead me to seek evidence. I value sources of evidence and social studies concepts as tools, as well as the answers they bring me. I think about past work I have done well, and how my attitudes change as I work. I set high goals for content learning. I notice differences among learners and help myself and others learn.
I am able to adapt and work collaboratively.	I flourish in an environment of trust. People learn more when they work together. I choose strategies to match social studies content and my goals. I know when I have reached my limit (or when others have) and change things when needed. I know when to focus and get down to work. My existing confidence in social studies successes can grow.
I use feedback to inform my teaching.	I know when feedback is needed on tasks, on process, on metacognition, and on personal identity. I use feedback to help me identify where I am going, how I will get there, and what to do next. I monitor and interpret teaching and learning "moves."

learning and teaching. Asking and answering questions about your own perceptions will help you learn more about yourself and help set goals for your long-term professional development—and this in turn will positively influence your practice.

Identity statements about learning apply equally to learners and teachers. Figure 2.2 presents some reflection questions that can guide self-assessment. Keeping track of your efforts through reflective journaling or conferences with an instructional coach can help ensure your continued success. Structure is vital to achievement of long-term goals.

Is My Teaching and Learning Transparent?

John Hattie (2012) stressed that both teachers and learners need to have access to the teacher's thinking. Our professional decisions about learning and instruction should follow the "open source" principle of free access to design: we should make our decisions and thinking explicit to students so they know what we are up to and what we hope to accomplish and so they can help with the decisions. We often require students to explain their thought processes, so we should ask the same of ourselves. Don't hide your thinking, your work! In Chapter 1, I discussed how providing students with time, choice, authentic outcomes, and self-selection of social settings supports joy in learning; these are also key areas for transparency in social studies.

Open sourcing your teaching also requires modeling the social studies engagement you would like to elicit from your students. In particular, ask yourself if you demonstrate for your students the affective skills that promote joyful learning:

- How strongly is my identity connected to questions and issues of social interaction?
- How do I model participation in public life?
- Do I model my own curiosity and interest by asking personal social studies questions and seeking evidence to investigate these?
- Do I actively monitor the match between my own skills and resources and the challenge of social studies content—and do I model this monitoring for my students?
- Do I model for students that I value understanding and inquiry as much as performance (scores, products)?
- How do I frame success and failure as integral parts of learning?
- Do I demonstrate perseverance in challenging tasks?

Assessing and Evaluating Texts and Materials

Because a joyful approach to social studies depends almost entirely on learners identifying and pursuing questions, anything that serves as evidence to answer students' questions is a "text." Artifacts count as well as books, and images that people "read" count as much as words (Draper et al., 2010). Repositories such as the Library of Congress hold millions of organized scanned primary source documents, including photos and film clips (visit the Primary Source Sets page at http://www.loc.gov/teachers/classroommaterials /primarysourcesets/). Many state museums have traveling boxes of artifacts to support specific topics, and families can provide realia to help students connect learning to personal experience. Three specific categories of texts and materials are central to joyful learning in social studies: manipulatives, authentic texts, and textbooks.

Manipulatives. Materials in social studies should support conceptual growth, not just demonstrate facts. Just as manipulatives are widely used to support student progress in learning math concepts, they can be incorporated in teaching social studies. Important foundational concepts in social studies include time, value, power, place and space, institution, and distribution. Manipulatives that allow students to create concrete, hands-on metaphors for the social world they are studying can support student understanding of these concepts. I

Images, realia, photos, film clips, artifacts, and manipulatives can help make content comprehensible for ELLs. Encouraging multiple forms of texts and ways to represent understandings will enhance ELL participation.

present some ideas for making abstract concepts concrete in Chapter 3.

Authentic texts. Asking and answering questions demands that students work with authentic texts such as primary sources, newspapers, vital records, demographic reports, infographics, maps, diagrams, and charts. We cannot address any area of study in adequate depth by solely relying on textbooks and workbooks—although these may form part of a scaffolding effort, helping students to build background knowledge and form questions. As students develop questions, our work turns to making authentic text accessible to students of varying reading abilities (see Chapter 3).

An ongoing part of our work as teachers is to help students approach text that is outside the range of what they might read independently; one way to do this is to model the excitement of finding just the right text. When students have a strong sense of purpose and specific questions to research, they are more likely to reach above their reading level for the answers; when students are engaged, they marshal all the problem-solving resources they have to make sense of a text (Kucer, 2009). To support students in this active literacy problem solving, we need to model and teach them how to identify and use good texts. To help teachers with this goal, the National Council for the Social Studies (NCSS) publishes a list of notable trade books each year categorized by social studies themes (see http://www.socialstudies.org/resources/notable).

Textbooks. Historian Matt Downey, coauthor of *Discover Colorado* (2007), emphasized to me that he, his coauthor, and his publisher all agreed that their textbook was intended as a classroom resource, not a curriculum. That is, textbooks are not an outline of everything you have to cover. Textbook authors try to be as inclusive as possible, providing background information on most topics that might be studied in school; they acknowledge that there is too much material in the textbook for a single school year. A joyful approach to social studies should free educators to use textbooks as one resource among many to support student learning.

A joyful approach to social studies allows for students to "read" anything that helps them build and answer their own questions. Authentic text is the core of this process; manipulatives help build metaphors and concepts students need to support ongoing discovery; textbooks and similar materials can give students a basic orientation to their study and help them form questions.

Consider sharing a variety of visual resources, and reading aloud from text you find engaging. When you find artifacts, maps, diagrams, primary sources, or other resources engaging, interpret these for students by thinking aloud. The teacher read-aloud is a time-tested strategy for modeling engagement, and one of the key practices in which teachers already experience much joy (Loyd, 2001). Why not turn this strategy to everyone's benefit in social studies as well?

Tests and Assessments

The word *assessment* has for too long signified only published, standardized tests. To be really useful, an assessment should tell us who our students are, what they can do, and what they know—so we know how and what to teach.

Tests usually provide just a tiny slice of this knowledge, and test data are meaningless unless integrated with classroom-based assessment tools.

In addition, engagement and purpose can trump established indexes of independent or instructional levels; engaged learners often will exceed their literacy abilities as derived from tests and inventories. Almost all authentic text will be challenging in some way; our job is to assist students in figuring out how to navigate texts to find and read the information they want and need, not to limit possible resources. Learning matters more than the demand that all reading be at the independent and instructional levels. Finding good evidence or exploring a good question should be celebrated as successful literacy moments and explicitly noticed for students as examples of their competence (e.g., "You were just reading a middle/high school/college-level text!").

Having purpose and asking and answering questions are two central tenets of the Common Core State Standards (CCSS) for informational text. The CCSS standards for K–12 social studies focus on inquiry and purpose, and being able to derive meaning from text. This means that we are free to design authentic assessments of content that matter to our students. The NCSS (2010) goal that social studies should prepare students to be active and engaged participants in public life (p. 210) can also guide our assessment efforts, in helping us to identify authentic outcomes.

Authentic assessments in social studies ask students to organize information, consider alternatives, demonstrate understanding, use methods of inquiry, elaborate, and connect to issues and audiences beyond the classroom walls (Todorov & Brousseau, 1998). This list of principles provides a structure for designing opportunities for students to demonstrate what they know, and in different ways; not all students will make a good showing when only one kind of assessment is offered. Consider experimenting with a menu of assessment options from which students can choose, selecting the methods they believe are most appropriate. If we follow the principle of expanding social studies units into much wider time frames, then there will be more degrees of freedom in formative assessment and more time for authenticity in summative ones.

Evaluating Schoolwide Configurations

In pursuing a joyful learning environment in social studies, you will need to evaluate how schoolwide configurations fit your school. Your ability to explain and demonstrate how a schoolwide effort correlates to contemporary demands (see Chapter 4) may determine how administrators respond.

Joyful learning in social studies does not occur in a vacuum; one thing to communicate with other school staff is how student success in social studies influences progress in other content areas. Social studies build background knowledge, vocabulary use, and ways of talking in academics. Social studies inquiry embodies many of the goals described in the CCSS. And, finally, remember that schools are authentic social studies settings: community institutions where basic understandings of civic competence are best understood by applying and practicing them.

Vertical and horizontal communication is essential to establishing a schoolwide joyful learning environment. Taylor, Pearson, Clark, and Walpole (2000) studied schools that beat the odds: high-achieving schools with low socioeconomic status. These schools found a sustainable model of teaching and learning that resulted in higher test scores as a by-product. Each of these schools had built a culture of communication, within and across grade levels. Teachers felt competent and engaged because of the ways they were connected to other teachers, students, and families. The importance of communication and connection is supported by research on effective professional development (Bean & Dagen, 2011; Beers, Beers, & Smith, 2009). Because teachers' feelings about their career are based on how connected they feel to the school as a whole, communication structures must work vertically (cross-grade and -subject) and horizontally (within-grade and -subject).

We should not be surprised that a well-organized school culture might lead to both joyful teaching and learning and high achievement scores. Pursuing a schoolwide climate of joy promises to pay dividends in teachers' view of their career and their daily work within the school.

Moving Forward in Social Studies

To get the most from joyful learning, we need to evaluate the essential elements that influence joyful learning: learners, teacher, texts and materials, assessments, and schoolwide configuration—and our evaluation must be guided by the key questions that keep the focus on the learner. Assessing each element supports implementation of the framework. In the next chapter I suggest some specific strategies and activities for joyful learning in the social studies classroom.

CHAPTER 3

Implementing Joyful Learning
in Social Studies

Academic subjects are abstract to most students, especially those in the early through middle school grades. Younger students don't see the connection between the classroom and the "real" world. With repeated exposure and explicit connections, older students are generally more aware of how academic subjects are related to work and life outside school. No matter their age, fostering students' personal connection to social studies is an essential step in helping them grasp and understand the world around them. Making explicit the connection between the learner and social studies serves to motivate and engage students.

In *Engaging Minds in the Classroom* (2014), Opitz and Ford presented a framework to help teachers purposefully select strategies and activities that promote joyful learning. The framework is rooted in research about motivation (see Chapter 1) and is applied in five key areas: school community, the physical environment (i.e., the classroom), whole-group instruction, small-group instruction, and individual instruction. Different activity structures can then be used within the framework to emphasize aspects of joyful learning. In this chapter, I offer some strategies and activities in each of these areas that enhance content knowledge while also increasing students' sense of belonging and learner identity.

School Community

Opitz and Ford (2014) stressed that a schoolwide identity is integral to creating a joyful learning environment. Through schoolwide activities, students understand that their school represents how communities outside schools work and how everyone in the community can work for the common good. Students often find high value in working as a community, which motivates them and sustains their engagement in the effort. Clear, attainable goals provide direction during engaged learning.

Social Action

The National Council for the Social Studies' (NCSS) position on social action is illustrated by its definition of social studies as a subject: the primary outcome for learners identified by NCSS (2010) is *civic competence*—knowledgeable participation in public life (p. 210). Social action projects both build school community and connect academic learning to the real world (Cole & McGuire, 2012). Without looking too far, a school community can find local concerns or causes that students feel invested in, whether it is focusing on issues such as conservation (Christie, Montgomery, & Staudt, 2012; McFadyen, 2012), communicating with the school board or elected officials about education initiatives, or something else entirely (e.g., Fry, Griffin, & Kirshner, 2012). The idea behind social action projects is for students to seek solutions to real-world problems that they can present to authentic audiences.

Schoolwide projects provide opportunities for ELLs to make connections to their community and develop a deeper sense of belonging, and may also lead to meaningful discussion regarding economic, cultural, and linguistic diversity.

Student-initiated responses to local problems embody value because students see and talk about how these problems affect their daily lives. Social action projects also demand focus and direction, and help build student skills in the areas of goal setting and attainment. Cooperation across grades and classrooms strengthens each student's identification with the school community.

It is this grassroots approach at the classroom level that gives us hope for schoolwide value for social action, and hope that students will value social action as adults.

Social action projects (Lewis, 1989, 1998) can be integrated with traditional classroom activities and with existing service learning initiatives. Service learning expands upon the general idea of community service to incorporate academic curriculum with meaningful service; visit the National Service-Learning Clearinghouse, http://www.servicelearning.org/, for more information. To identify potential projects, model for students how to connect universal human themes and concerns to local issues. Water, land, power, and people are good places to start; follow up with questions that guide students to apply broad ideas to the community. You can link read-aloud (or students' free-reading selections) or study units to real-world sources of information on social action questions (e.g., a project on whales and whaling leads to exploring the International Whaling Commission). Modeling and discussing how to locate and explore resources also provides an opportunity to support and build students' digital literacy (Lee, 2004).

Here are the basic types of social action projects and activities:

• *Local inquiry projects*, in which students identify issues in the immediate community. They then research people, policies, and practices that surround these issues.

• *Advocacy and communication activities*, in which students research education issues and organize and advocate for their own learning, via petitions, proposals, public service announcements, social networks, phone calls, town halls, debates, hearings, and information presentations.

• *Governance research and experiences*, during which students investigate decision making surrounding a local issue, including laws at the local, state, and national levels. Mock trials, court visits, and conflict resolution structures in school give students close experience with the procedural aspects of public life.

• *Community resources research*, with students identifying local advocacy and social action groups, lobbying concerns, agencies, clubs, and civic or nonprofit organizations (see Filipovitch & Ozturk, 2012).

Matching Outcomes to Authentic Audiences

A social action project offers opportunities for students to develop writing and presentation skills suited to different audiences—that is, *authentic outcomes*. Authenticity comes from creating outcomes typically sought out or needed by real audiences. Preparing products for authentic audiences lends a sense of relevance and urgency to students' work in social studies and encourages them to become active participants in public life. Authentic audiences and outcomes provide students with social opportunities that increase their self-efficacy, and students also gain a sense of competence when their efforts look like those of experts. Figure 3.1 provides a matrix for matching different types of outcomes or products to authentic audiences. Offering students multiple ways to present their knowledge throughout the year enhances attribution and control beliefs:

- Secondary school students develop impact statements, white papers, or FAQs to summarize findings on an issue for policy makers or nonprofit organizations;
- High school students develop voting bluebooks describing ballot initiatives and candidate positions for their newly registered peers;
- A schoolwide infographic project (timelines, charts, slide show presentations, posters) provides all students with a comprehensive view on a single issue or topic;
- Students debate a topic before a panel of experts; and
- Students from different classrooms or grades develop pages for a joint website to be used to educate other partners or teams of students.

In developing authentic outcomes, tailor instruction to match students' grade level and interests. For younger students, spend plenty of time examining models of authentic outcomes before trying to produce them. Provide menus of choices for outcomes, or provide templates that allow students to stay focused on content.

For older students, more complicated outcomes should incorporate formative checkpoints, structured to help them keep track of what they have done and to plan and ensure they meet goals. For example, in a project that

FIGURE 3.1 Social Action: Matching Authentic Outcomes to Authentic Audiences								
	Audience							
Outcome	Social networks	Policy makers	Community organizations	Panel of experts	Younger/older students	Peer students	Partners or teams	Family and friends
Debate								
Impact statement								
White paper or FAQ								
Voting "bluebook"								
Simulated government								
Documentary video								
Exhibits								
Performances								
Website								
Infographics								
Informational book								

spans six weeks, students might be accountable for formative checks of work at the end of each week.

Classroom Environment

The classroom environment strongly influences how students identify themselves as learners. In the social studies classroom, it is important to incorporate demonstrations of civic competence; in so doing, the classroom mirrors

Providing a safe classroom community environment where students feel comfortable to communicate will lower their affective filter and in turn enhance ELLs' second-language acquisition opportunities (Krashen, 1987).

the outside world in its expectation of participation in the public sphere. Providing students an opportunity for control and ownership, allowing them to assist in structuring the nature of the school day or class period, makes them active participants in their learning and builds a sense of community. It also encourages students to attribute success and failure to their own effort, rather than to luck or other factors, including the teacher.

Long-Term Inquiry Learning

Inquiry learning discourages a passive view of schoolwork; instead, learning is driven by students' wonder. In inquiry learning, students set a "journey" goal rather than a "destination" goal: to find a sustainable question that will lead them to powerful sources of information. This experience bolsters their confidence and competence in learning to explore and make sense of the information they discover along the way. Allowing students to develop questions to guide their learning, and supporting their pursuit of these questions, supports motivation and engagement. The inquiry journey is a circular process, where discovery leads to further investigation (see Figure 3.2).

A few years ago, I was part of a team investigating how to engage learners suffering from long-term disengagement, low achievement, and even open disdain for school (Erekson, High, & Baldwin, 2005). Our research led us to believe that the key was twofold: focusing all instructional decisions on transfer and engagement, and giving students a range of choices under a broad teacher-selected social studies theme, one that could support diverse avenues of inquiry (e.g., social structures, rights and responsibilities, conflict, civil rights, political structures, law, economics, art and architecture, cultural identity, environment; see NCSS, 2010, Chapter 2). Implementing this approach was successful: half of the students scored above the school's standardized test growth norms and the standard deviation (Erekson et al., 2005). The main change we had made was

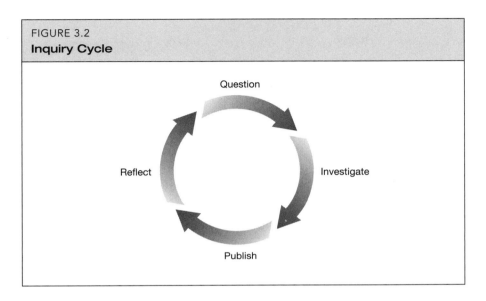

FIGURE 3.2
Inquiry Cycle

Question

Reflect

Investigate

Publish

a shift that enabled us to think about inquiry as a large umbrella, with skills and strategies underneath.

The change was a long-term process. It can take months for students to demonstrate the vocabulary and other language gains afforded by deep inquiry. I have designed entire semesters around a chosen topic, and one of my classes once researched a topic for a whole year. To establish a classroom environment that supports long-term inquiry, it is important to incorporate authentic outcomes, collaborative options for studying and reading, formative assessment checkpoints, and learning and literacy strategies students can use.

Supporting year-long inquiry requires different types of scaffolding for different grade levels. For elementary school students,

- Teach students where to find and how to use sources of information.
- Use teacher read-aloud to assist in literacy tasks.
- Involve students in determining research topics by voting from a menu of options.
- Use guided reading and other grouping structures to provide students with support in reading and using technology sources to support their inquiry.

For middle and high school students, continue to identify and share how to find and use sources of information, but vary groupings (e.g., paired reading, collaborative groups) as a social structure to develop social strengths in inquiry. Encourage students to use inquiry questions to push toward social action and service learning.

Creating a Classroom Social System

Creating a classroom token economy strengthens individual students' identification as being part of a community of learners. Any historical period, any place in the world, any social structure that might hold interest for students can provide the structure for a social system. A classroom social system might mirror the European feudal system, Shogun-era Japan, Han China, Pharaoh-dynasty Egypt, or Incan or Aztec culture. Other teachers have used nautical, military, or U.S. government roles to provide a structure for a class culture. My 5th grade teacher implemented a full municipal economy, with a city government, postal service, and salaries to be earned and spent. It was one of the most memorable years in my school experience.

> Choice in inquiry can facilitate ownership, metacognition, and enhanced use of sophisticated literacy practices. Motivation is enhanced through choice as students simultaneously develop deeper content knowledge and acquire English (Guccione, 2011).

Having students participate in choosing a social system will increase their engagement. Many students are already familiar with social structures, from their experience in computer role-playing and video games. Don't be surprised if your students in middle and high school already have developed personal interest in and knowledge of other societies and cultures.

Another idea is to seek input from students' families. You can structure the class system based on families' background knowledge and cultural connections. Or a parent who is an avid Revolutionary War reenactor might be eager to assist in designing a classroom structure mirroring the eighteenth-century military.

There are a few guidelines for successfully implementing a classroom social system:

• Promote learners through ranks in the society based on an economy of merit. Decide what will count as a value.

• Link the value system for promotion and the actual roles of the ranks to civic competence values, such as service. Issue challenges that students can use to provide evidence of civic competence. (Note that rank promotions should be earned separately from grades.)

• Link promotion to efforts above and beyond normal academic expectations. Linking promotion to effort (as a part of and apart from class assignments) provides students an opportunity to accomplish something within their control.

• Give the roles real significance. Students with rank might have freedoms to make decisions and choices (e.g., working individually or in a group, choosing free time activities, selecting topics of study, and selecting outcomes to work toward).

Whole-Group Instruction

A frequent lament among social studies teachers is that learners need more background knowledge—but what do we mean by "background knowledge"? To effectively absorb and understand new information, students need opportunities to use their everyday knowledge as hooks between the new academic content and what already exists in their lives. Connecting each student's contributions to academic knowledge gives students a sense that they are both able and good at social studies. Whole-group instruction activities should encourage every student to participate and contribute.

Students' connection and memory are likely to be stronger when new information is presented using visuals, and when hands-on activities encourage them to make abstract ideas concrete. Both of these strategies are entwined with value; involving visual modalities and building on student interest increases the time and effort students are willing to invest in learning.

Visual Experiences

Visual experiences can both introduce new concepts and give students opportunities to make connections with background knowledge using everyday language. For this activity, provide pairs or small groups of students with different sets of images and videos on a single theme or relating to a particular unit of study. Over the course of a couple of days, students review and compare the images, recording their impressions using outlines, graphic organizers, or notes. Encourage students to explore new terminology and vocabulary relating to the images, or to investigate related events. At the end of the week, have students share their observations during a whole-class discussion. At this point, assist students in developing summative analysis and critical thinking about the images (e.g., the "L" in KWL, semantic feature analysis, compare/contrast, description, cause/effect, inferences).

A word of caution: too many images in a session results in lost engagement. Use the old neurology principle for new learning: low duration, high intensity, and high frequency (Doman, 1966). This means only a few minutes of an activity, with extremely intense and fast presentation, but repeated many times across a few days (*high frequency* means it can even be repeated within a single day several times, as long as there is a true time lapse between sessions).

Concrete Concepts

Whatever concept we hope for learners to internalize needs to be enacted physically and socially (Vygotsky, 1986). Concepts develop over time—weeks and months, rather than in single lessons or one school day. Learners need repeated opportunities for application. The concreteness of physical handling and interpersonal activity provides students with metaphors for concepts (Lakoff & Johnson, 2003) and thus enhances learning.

One activity that can help students build concepts is to create a hands-on, visual timeline. You can build a timeline around the walls of the classroom using twine and index cards, or rolls of butcher-block paper; for middle and high school students, consider using an online program or software to create an ongoing, interactive project. Incorporating students' family histories in this project can be helpful, across grade levels. For younger students, using their own families' experiences as a basis for discussing past and present provides a basic understanding of chronology. For older students, using family histories can help them see themselves as part of history. Incorporating points of reference (e.g., grandparents' birthdays; family's immigration to the United States; inventions of pop culture items such as Barbie dolls, Legos, iPods) and scale helps students talk in terms of known lengths of time. Using the visual of the timeline, students' scale of reference can be expanded to centuries. Link students' knowledge of current technology to a period prior to its invention. For example, "We can fly 3,000 miles across the country in six hours, but before cars and airplanes the trip would have taken months on horseback or in covered wagons." Or, "Before the Internet, before the telephone, and before mail delivery to small islands, soldiers who didn't have radios went months or years before learning World War II was over."

Concrete concept activities are an example of comprehensible input, an essential component of sheltered instruction (Echevarria, Short, & Vogt, 2011), which assists in making content and language accessible for ELLs.

An interactive timeline is just one way to use concrete, hands-on activities to support student acquisition of abstract concepts. Figure 3.3 suggests some other classroom activities for different grade levels.

Small-Group Instruction

Small-group instruction uses social interaction and collective responsibility to empower students as social studies learners. Assigning students to small groups allows each individual to work at an appropriate yet challenging level. Students also can work on common or individual weaknesses and share information and skills with one another, while focusing on a shared topic of interest within social studies.

Reading Social Studies Texts

Small groups allow social studies teachers to provide students with direct instruction in how to read social studies texts. As discussed in Chapter 2, to engage students we need to work with authentic texts—but almost all authentic text will be challenging in some way to most learners. We want to encourage learners to approach texts of all types as part of their ongoing inquiry. In small groups, teachers can show students how to find and focus on small,

FIGURE 3.3

Concrete Concepts: Activities by Grade Level

Grade Level	Activity	Concept	Concrete Concept: Manipulative or Simulation
Elementary school	Metronome steps	Speed of travel	With a metronome, students take one step for each beat as they move toward a goal. For foot travel, heel-to-toe walking; for early motor travel, a regular pace; for high-speed travel, giant steps.
	Whale to scale	Scale, labor division	With garbage bags and tape, create a shell the size of a real whale. Students get underneath and hold hands. Other students try to pull this whale to conceptualize towing it from the ocean to shore.
	Modeling clay opportunity	Opportunity cost	Set up a barter system of goods made of modeling clay or dough. Learners experience opportunity cost as prioritizing desires in limited distribution.
Middle school	Circular flow simulation	Circular flow of resources and costs	A classroom of tables or desks can mirror circular flow between households and firms. Tokens represent resources, capital, and labor. Expand for government, financial, and service sectors.
	Time change	Historical change in material culture	Students locate images on a theme and present in backward time order (e.g., modern cruise ship/Renaissance sailing ship/Viking ship; modern house/beam and wattle house/post and thatch house; modern cooking pot/iron cauldron/ earthen pot/stone boiler).
	Traveling trunk/ archaeology dig box (Chisholm, Leone, & Bentley, 2007)		Students collect or create and display artifacts related to a specific event or time period.
High school	Living history		Students design classroom-based reenactments and living history sites (see Daniels, 2010).
	Walk through history		Pairs of students each research a decade of the same century; the class as a whole combines individual projects as a "walk-through" timeline of events.

essential passages—"hooks"—which in turn can help them navigate texts as a whole.

When first introducing this strategy, select hook passages on the basis of potential interest to students; this will allow you to model intrinsic motivation for them. Highlighting the hook passage is a tool for engendering interest in content and encouraging engagement in learning context. Questions about the hook passage lead learners to other passages for answers, sustaining interest and promoting engagement—part of the inquiry cycle. Understanding the hook passage provides a basis for goals in understanding less interesting content, which can be prompted with questions that connect to the interesting passage. Providing learners with rewritten passages and originals side by side allows them to see an immediate goal in mastering academic language.

> Instruction surrounding nonfiction text features such as illustrations, labels, captions, diagrams, charts, and graphs can help ELLs construct meaning with text before they are able to independently decode the entire text.

When students realize that they can approach a text without being put off by complex sentences and vocabulary, they begin to believe that their perceptions of ability and competence are not static but can adapt to meet the demands of different types of material. Learning to read informational text in a way that bends text format and structure to fit their needs as learners (highlighting linked content and ideas, rather than reading directly from top to bottom) gives them another skill set and promotes self-efficacy. In the process, they are learning to use everyday language to help them toward the academic reading. Figure 3.4 presents the steps for directly teaching students to approach differing levels of social studies texts using hook passages.

As students grow in age, reading ability, and content knowledge, teachers can broaden selection of hook passages, introducing longer and more varied texts. When modeling rewriting for older students, retain more general academic terms and focus on rewriting texts using specialized topical language.

FIGURE 3.4 Direct Instruction in Reading Social Studies Texts		
Step	**Skill**	**Scaffolding**
1. Find the hook passage	Identify the main idea in a passage	• Point out interesting facts, well-told stories, or topics relevant to students. • Teach previewing strategies (skim to identify unfamiliar words or terms; investigate these to enhance understanding). • Use variations on teacher read-aloud, partner reading, and paired reading. • Use reciprocal questioning to encourage ongoing comprehension. • Use discussion to connect the hook passage to prior knowledge.
2. Reorganize around the hook passage	Build background knowledge and connections to content	• Read the hook passage in the context of surrounding passages to provide context. • Ask journalistic questions (i.e., *who, what, when, where, why,* and *how*). • Number passages that provide the clearest answers to questions from the hook passage, to model how to navigate texts out of order. • Identify out-of-order reading as a new skill set.
3. Reword or rewrite the hook passage	Relate new content to existing knowledge and vocabulary	• Model how to reword the hook passage, using basic principles about vocabulary substitution and sentence simplification (use technology aids as needed and appropriate). Use vocabulary similar to students' everyday usage. • Compare the rewritten passage with the original and highlight new content or information.

Developing Critical Thinking

Many students think that expertise is based on innate talent rather than effort and learning. Making "expert" thinking explicit is a basic tenet of control belief. As in inquiry learning, we must help students seek questions that sustain thorough investigation, rather than questions with easy answers.

Asking students to think as experts builds their critical thinking skills and confidence as social studies learners. Students develop questions that expert thinkers might posit; groups can be assigned the general categories of political scientists, economists, geographers, and historians. In a three-year project with an urban school district in Colorado, I collaborated with researchers in each of these four disciplines to find entry points to the standards. After identifying central concepts in the standards, we converted these into categories of questions students could use as tools to guide developing their own expert questions (see Figure 3.5). The most fundamental questions come first; the deeper students go in each list, the more the questions encourage critical thinking—inquiring about processes and purposes that underlie social interactions of all kinds.

The set of questions is adaptable to any topic and is easily adapted to existing curriculum or to open-ended independent inquiry projects. For example, students studying the White River War (see Downey & Bliss, 2008) might ask, specifically, what was the opportunity cost both for Meeker and for the Utes when Meeker decided to plow up the Utes' horse field? How would knowing these things help explain how and why the war broke out?

When modeling the process for students, use everyday language to help students gain the power and competence of experts who use specialized vocabulary. Also, encourage students to think across topics in social studies. For example, with the Greensboro, North Carolina, sit-ins as a topic in a civil rights unit, learners might start with questions about power, then move to questions of how freedom to enter a restaurant is an economic matter of decision making (What is the scarce resource?), then to how this freedom was distributed differently across race and geography and when this all happened.

Small-group work should be reinforced by a whole-class activity. After different expert groups present their questions, the whole class might discuss and identify connected answers (or additional questions for inquiry). Reinforce student identification with professionals in these fields by arranging field trips to historical sites or Skype conferences or classroom visits from specialists in different fields, or show videos of experts in action. Documentary films are filled with expert commentary, which provides a springboard for class discussion and further inquiry.

Individual Instruction

Individual projects should be included in any menu of instructional strategies in the social studies classroom, providing students with opportunities to

FIGURE 3.5			
Thinking Like an Expert			
What would a geographer ask?		**What would a historian ask?**	
Location	Where is the place?	Frame of reference	What questions can you ask about the past?
Condition	What is the place?	Evidence	What evidence do you need to answer your questions?
Connection	How is this place linked to others?	Time order	Can you arrange events in order? Does this help explain why and how things happened?
Region	How are nearby places like this one?	Social order	Can you explain how people lived together in the past? How did this change over time?
Analog	How are faraway places like this one?	Science, tools, and work	How have these changed over time?
Aura	How does one place affect its neighbors?	Politics and government	How did these change over time? Why?
Comparison	How are places alike and different?	Ideas and beliefs	How did these change over time? Why?
Pattern	Are there groups, sets, or other patterns?		
Correlation	How are some of the patterns alike?		
Gradient	What is it like as we go between places?		
Diffusion	How do things spread out in the land?		
Hierarchy	How does the place fit with other places (town > state > country)?		
What would an economist ask?		**What would a political scientist ask?**	
Decision making	Who decides how to use scarce resources?	Power	Who has it? Who doesn't? How does one get it? What do people do with it?
Cost/benefit	What is the cost of deciding something? What are the benefits of deciding something? To whom? Who decides what to do about cost and benefits?	Choice	Who decides and chooses, and who doesn't? How do people decide and choose? What helps people decide and choose?
Options	What other ways are there to use resources? Have people tried those ways?	Values	What is important? Is there a plan? Who decides what counts as important? When, where, and how do things happen?
Influences	Do people make decisions based on price, government, or tradition?	Beliefs	What are people being talked into? How do people get us to believe in their plans? What do we really care about? Do these match?
Commerce	What is traded? Is it money or other resources? Why and how does trade happen? How does trading show that people depend on each other?		

make connections and contribute. As Opitz and Ford (2014) noted, individual instruction is perhaps one of the best ways to address and encourage student interest and choice, which in turn motivates learners. Individual instruction allows students to choose and explore topics of interest, and individualized projects encourage engaged, independent student learning. Individual learning experiences can help to build confidence and self-reliance, and stretch your students to perform in areas that they might choose to avoid in a group setting.

Visual Essays

When I discussed visual experiences as a teaching strategy for whole-group instruction, I noted that the process helps make abstract concepts concrete for students and assists them in connecting knowledge to their own experience. The same principle applies when designing lessons that ask students to convert abstract ideas into visual presentations. As an extended example of an authentic outcome, the visual essay works primarily on intrinsic motivation, while making use of the general human preference for processing information visually (Medina, 2008). Visual essay projects also play to the appeal of visual media to today's learners and to the visual strengths most students have from their life experience as visual learners. Framing concepts visually requires students to limit information to essential points, although it also encourages them to consider and ask questions about what is not pictured. In addition, creating visual presentations allows students to demonstrate competence traditionally presented in written work, but which incorporates different skills. The ability to be good at creating a visual essay depends less on linguistic competence and more on thinking structure; recognizing that they have this particular strength bolsters students' self-efficacy.

Thompson and Williams (2008) equipped students with cameras when visiting historic sites on a field trip. Students prepared for the trip by thinking about what kinds of images would be important to them and would help others understand what happened at the site. Their resulting photo essays reflected each individual student's perspective and value of the information at the site.

This idea can be adapted in a couple of different ways, depending on the ages, skills, and interests of your students. You can, of course, follow Thompson and Williams's format and have students create photo essays following a field trip (allow students to use their smart phones or camera-enabled tablets; you can supply disposable cameras if necessary). Another idea is to expand the idea of the visual essay: individual students could create posters, informational booklets or books, slideshows, or digital videos (with music) to represent information, concepts, and ideas relating to a unit of study. Again, offering students a menu of choices for the project engages their interest and spurs enthusiasm.

Engaging learners in this project, however, still means encouraging the use of thought structures in their presentations: description, sequencing, cause-effect, problem-solution, and compare-contrast. At all grade levels, teachers must model the process and provide mentor texts for teaching the principles of essay building. Limiting students' projects to a certain number of images, slides, or amount of time (for videos) requires them to think through which combination of images will best represent the topic. Visual essays are a persuasive genre, and the complexity of what learners want audiences to think and feel when "reading" the essay should determine the presentation style. Having students present their essays and discuss them will help them grow in verbal and oral thought structures.

Exploring Universal Experiences

Questions are doorways into exploration, and thinking about the evidence and information the question demands is the path to the other side. When students ask their own questions, they set their own goals; this is much more likely to lead to engaged learning than teacher- or textbook-authored questioning. Learning to use a survey-questioning technique (e.g., Robinson, 1970; see summary at http://www.studygs.net/texred2.htm) requires students to locate important parts in a text (such as headers and topic sentences) and recast these as questions, using their own words. Combining this technique with asking and answering questions about cultural and affective universal experiences strengthens students' social studies content knowledge and ability to make connections.

George Murdock (1945) identified common human activity across history and cultures. I have also encouraged students to identify *affective* universals using folklore (see Thompson, 1966) and anthropology—traditional tales are a common source of human experience. Universals are engaging because they represent expectations of existing background knowledge. As students survey content materials, they can use cultural and affective universals as a menu for crafting questions, or for extending and elaborating on questions (see Figure 3.6).

This activity requires both learner and teacher to focus on finding something powerfully human. It also encourages students to use questions as critical thinking tools for examining materials and texts. To model the process for students, read aloud a passage and identify an aspect of the human experience featured in the text. Rework the topic into a question about the text and engage students in a discussion. Focus on cultural and affective universal experiences, asking *how* and *why* questions that require elaboration and thinking. Having students consider and discuss their own experience builds connections with social studies content.

FIGURE 3.6	
Universals: What Is the Human Experience?	
Affective Universals *How do people experience the following?*	**Cultural Universals** *How do people experience the following?*
Belonging (invited, uninvited) Fear and security Interment and containment Trust and belief Individual choice and society's expectations Investment of time and life Value of objects and people Changing poverty and wealth Getting into and escaping from danger Cleverness, wisdom, foolishness, stupidity Fairness and injustice Loyalty and betrayal Privacy Reversals in situation	Food Clothing Shelter Communication Transportation Family living Government Money Childhood Roles for women and men Status Wealth and poverty Achievement or merit Entertainment Animals

As Opitz and Ford (2014) noted, combining individual instruction or independent study with whole-class discussion and review after a project is completed reinforces students' identification with the classroom as a community of learners. It is also important to incorporate student self-evaluation; having students reflect on what they did well, what they learned or accomplished, what they might improve next time, and what else they want to explore promotes ongoing learning and content mastery.

In this chapter and those that preceded it, I have illustrated how the framework for joyful learning can be implemented in social studies classrooms. The diverse opportunities afforded by the areas of learning, including within a school community, classroom environment, whole group, small group, and individually, can spark self-awareness in your students. From there, capitalizing on their strengths and working on their weaknesses can profoundly affect the level of joy you and your students find in the classroom.

I recognize, however, that you might have some lingering questions about how the joyful learning approach fits with other initiatives and expectations that frame your teaching environment. In Chapter 4, I address some common concerns about implementing an innovative approach such as joyful learning within existing education structures.

Using Joyful Learning to Support Education Initiatives

Whether it is a change in federal law, such as the revision to the Individuals with Disabilities Education Act in 2004 that spurred use of Response to Intervention (RTI); the introduction of new standards such as the Common Core State Standards (CCSS) and the College, Career, and Civic Life (C3) framework; or something as broad as the United States' evolving linguistic and cultural diversity, teachers often feel the effects of external demands on their teaching day. In fact, many teachers have cited these external demands as reasons for accepting early retirement incentives or switching careers (Kopkowski, 2008). The authors and editors of the *Engaging Minds* books recognize that contemporary demands are a fact of teaching life; in pursuing a joyful learning environment, teachers need to be able to manage outside demands as well as manage their classrooms. The "Yeah, but . . ." questions (Opitz & Ford, 2008) surrounding implementing an innovative teaching strategy in the midst of other requirements can stall progress. It is possible, however, to respond to education initiatives and also keep our eyes on the prize—joyful learning.

How Can Joyful Learning Be Implemented Within RTI Frameworks?

RTI is a mechanism that can be used to more accurately identify students with learning disabilities or those otherwise in need of support. RTI often focuses on providing specialized support in three tiers, based on how students respond to research-based instructional interventions. Just as high-quality universal instruction forms the base of all RTI models, the instructional approaches described in this book are well grounded in research. The joyful learning framework, based on motivational generalizations and incorporating strategies in key areas as a result of assessment of environmental elements, aligns with RTI principles (International Reading Association, 2010; see Figure 4.1).

A major theme in RTI is that teachers' professional growth matters most (Allington, 2008). When students don't respond to a particular instructional approach, teachers need to know how to tailor it or how to select another approach. Without this ability to shift, it is not students who fail to respond; it is the interventions that fail to reach students. When programs and plans reach their limits, teachers who know how to adapt their instruction are the greatest RTI asset.

As I mentioned in the Introduction, interventions that ignore affective (noncognitive) processes often fall short of their goals. Emotion, attitude, identity, and interests hold a kind of governing influence on cognitive thinking. Many teachers know that the underlying reasons for disengagement are often related to a student's perceptions of failure and risk, yet they continue to use tools that address only the cognitive aspects of learning. Methods and techniques that address affective thinking must become part of our toolkit if we are to embrace the best interpretation of RTI. A joyful mindset for teaching social studies will help us make clear connections to our students' affective selves, in turn helping them discover the human interest that pervades social studies but that is not often emphasized in school.

How Does Joyful Learning Address Achievement Gaps?

Keith Stanovich (1986) wrote about the achievement gap in terms of the Matthew Effect, using the biblical story of the wise and foolish servant to explain the irony that those who already have much tend to get more, while those who already have little tend to get less. This applies to student motivation as well as to knowledge. When students have repeated opportunities to

FIGURE 4.1
Correlation of Joyful Learning Framework to RTI Principles

RTI Principle	Joyful Learning in Social Studies
Instruction Instruction needs to be of the highest quality and engage students.	The framework in social studies encourages students to ask questions, and then seek evidence from authentic texts. Inquiry learning of this sort is research based and engaging for learners.
Responsive teaching and differentiation Teacher-student interaction should guide selection of instructional techniques and materials.	The joyful learning framework incorporates use of student interest inventories to help guide instructional development; in addition, suggested strategies and activities include demonstrations of topics, reading aloud, collaborative work, and choice, all of which require teacher-student interaction.
Assessment Assessment needs to be multidimensional.	Social studies assessment is varied and occurs in authentic learning contexts.
Collaboration All professionals work together to bring forth the best learning climate for the entire school community.	The joyful learning framework requires collaboration with other educators and demonstration of student learning for authentic audiences within the school. Successful approaches are shared through these demonstrations, co-teaching, and peer coaching. The framework requires teachers to build on the strengths of individual students, and scaffold learning as needed to support mastery.
Systematic and comprehensive approaches A schoolwide model that encompasses a systematic approach to assessment and instruction is essential.	The framework requires assessing schoolwide configurations and promoting joyful learning throughout the school community. Joyful learning is assumed to be dependent on an overall systematic approach.
Expertise The teacher is the core of effective learning.	Teachers' professional development and engagement are essential to student growth and to joyful learning. The joyful learning framework includes teacher modeling of strategies, identification of self as learner, and other techniques that build teacher-student relationships and motivate and engage learners.

view themselves as competent, they get more competent. When they have repeated chances to view themselves as less competent, they grow to believe and behave according to this narrative of diminishing competence. Learners who are strongly motivated want to learn more, whereas those with little affective strength often get less motivated by interventions teachers offer.

Slowing down the curriculum for students who do not show the quickest competence is sometimes seen as the way to help students learn. As well intended as this effort seems, it more often than not results in a holding pattern of repeated slow instruction that lasts for years. Closing the gap on a curve cannot happen with steady, linear progress. Progress must speed up! To help students make large gains over short time, we need to develop an acceleration mindset:

• Focus efforts on transfer and acceleration, not on self-contained programs or incremental skills remediation.

• Use choice and motivation, but within limits: provide students a menu of options from which to choose their materials, questions, and subtopics.

• When selecting topics, choose those filled with human interest that can sustain months of long-term inquiry into subtopics.

• Guide students to select and practice reading strategies that will help them feel less frustrated as well as help them derive content from what they read.

• Prompt students to transfer what they learn to other courses and to the tests they take, so that growth in one content area leads to growth in another.

All these principles are incorporated in the joyful learning framework and have the potential to close achievement gaps.

How Does Joyful Learning Correlate to New Standards of Learning?

The CCSS (National Governors Association Center for Best Practices, Council of Chief State School Officers, 2010), the National Curriculum Standards for Social Studies (NCSS, 2010), and the C3 framework (NCSS, 2013) provide guidance for teaching concepts more deeply, helping students to identify relationships between different topics and build connections between academic content and the real world. Throughout this book I have discussed how joyful learning correlates to the NCSS curriculum standards; it is important to understand as well that neither the CCSS nor C3 framework represents a conflict with this approach. In fact, Opitz and Ford's (2014) joyful learning framework provides a way for teachers to meet the goals of these nationwide standards for social studies.

The CCSS focus on results rather than means, integrated literacy skills, research and media skills, and coherence in instruction and assessment is reflected throughout my discussion of the essence of joyful learning and its classroom strategies. The CCSS describes college- and career-ready students as those who demonstrate independence, have built content knowledge, can integrate knowledge and ideas, can develop responses for authentic audiences, have developed comprehension and critiquing skills, value evidence, and understand other perspectives and cultures (National Governors Association Center for Best Practices, 2010, pp. 7, 10). These skills are encouraged by the joyful learning approach.

The C3 framework was developed to help teachers guide students in growing to "recognize societal problems; ask good questions and develop robust investigations into them; consider possible solutions and consequences; separate evidence-based claims from parochial opinions; and communicate and act upon what they learn" (NCSS, 2013, p. 6). C3 was developed to correlate to the CCSS, and its educational principles are categorized into four dimensions:

- Developing questions and planning inquiries;
- Applying disciplinary concepts and tools;
- Evaluating sources and using evidence; and
- Communicating conclusions and taking informed action.

Again, all these areas are focal points in the joyful learning framework.

Within the scope of my 20 years of experience, the teachers who have fared the best are those who work actively with existing standards. In addition to informing practice, standards guide discussions of education with parents, colleagues, and administrators. Standards provide a framework within which we as teachers can communicate *what we really do as professional teachers*. Referencing standards when you speak and write about your strengths as a teacher, and when you discuss your efforts to develop a joyful learning environment, will enhance others' understanding. To help structure this discussion, review the standards while considering what you know about joyful learning. Note areas of correlation and identify how the joyful learning framework meets the expectations, and use this knowledge when you speak about your teaching practice and principles.

As teachers, we are not used to using standards to advocate for ourselves. Self-advocacy may be new territory for many of us, because we did not expect it to be part of the job description way back when we decided to become teachers. My advice is to follow your inclination to teach for joy and to reflect on elements within reform movements that correlate to joyful principles. Accepting this charge to be a teacher-leader in using the standards is part of keeping on the track that leads to joyful learning and to a joyful *career*.

How Does Joyful Learning Support the Focus on Accountability and Assessment?

The current wave of accountability has people focused on teacher quality, partly because research has shown that high student achievement is correlated to individual teachers' expertise and ability (Wright, Horn, & Sanders, 1997). This means that the qualities teachers bring to work every day are the most important factors in student growth. On the one hand, recognizing this has led to a trend against using student test scores to "grade" schools (Ravitch, 2010). However, arguing against misuses of standardized testing is of little benefit if teachers do not have a positive counterweight to recommend.

Along with all the rhetoric on testing, there has been a consistent undercurrent of rational educators arguing for a variety of authentic, classroom-based assessment instruments (Flurkey, 2006; Johnston, 1997). Perhaps even more compelling is the notion that assessment should be used to discover students' learning strengths. Nations where assessment is working well for teachers and learners are those where assessment practices support learning instead of evaluating it. These countries are trying to capture and capitalize the spirit of creativity and flexibility that has long been a trademark of learners in the

United States (Sahlberg & Hargreaves, 2011; Zhao, 2009). So, in the wider world in which we live, there are many willing to join you in the conversation about what effective assessment really is.

The path to joyful teaching is not completely devoid of frustrating bumps in the road. Our growth as teachers often depends on us facing up to challenges to our professionalism. The current accountability and assessment movements may present teachers with many of these contradictions and frustrations. However, a teacher interested in crafting a joyful career must learn to find ways to serve students, and that may mean reinventing our view of assessment.

Conclusion

Contemporary demands are literally that: the demands of our current time. Although many teachers find these demands and influences frustrating, teachers who focus on joyful learning are able to move forward with reasonable demands and to move forward in spite of unreasonable ones. As teachers, we need to be ready to interpret these demands in favor of our students and ourselves.

History holds parallel lessons for us as teachers (and particularly as social studies teachers). Although most of the discussion surrounding development of the Declaration of Independence in the late 1700s focused on the clear list of grievances against England, there was also a consistent core of abolitionists in the public background who focused their thinking on the document's guarantees of universal freedom and inalienable rights—including *pursuit of happiness* (Slauter, 2011). Frederick Douglass recognized decades later that the country had only given lip service to these rights despite a long tradition of open celebrations of American freedom. What does this mean as we move forward with our efforts to establish joyful learning environments? Others may get distracted by a narrow reading of policy or get caught up in the fervor of the latest reform movement, but our focus as joyful learning advocates is consistent with democratic beliefs and values. We know that our students will do their best work in strong pursuit of happiness . . . and we will do our best work as well.

References

Allington, R. L. (2008). *What really matters in response to intervention: Research-based designs.* New York: Pearson.

ASCD. (2007). *The learning compact redefined: A call to action. A report of the commission on the whole child.* Alexandria, VA: Author. Retrieved from http://www.ascd.org/ASCD/pdf/Whole%20Child/WCC%20Learning%20Compact.pdf

Bean, R., & Dagen, A. (2011). *Best practices of literacy leaders: Keys to school improvement.* New York: Guilford.

Beers, C., Beers, J., & Smith, J. (2009). *A principal's guide to literacy action.* New York: Guilford.

Brophy, J., & Alleman, J. (2007). *Powerful social studies for elementary students* (2nd ed.). Belmont, CA: Wadsworth.

Chisholm, A. G., Leone, M. P., & Bentley, B. (2007). Archaeology in the classroom: Using a dig box to understand the past. *Social Education, 71,* 272–277.

Christie, E. M., Montgomery, S. E., & Staudt, J. (2012). Little by little: Global citizenship through local action inspired by Wangari Maathai. *Social Studies and the Young Learner, 25*(2), 8–11.

Cole, B., & McGuire, M. (2012). Real-world problems: Engaging young learners in critical thinking. *Social Studies and the Young Learner, 24*(4), 15–17.

Daniels, M. L. (2010). A living history classroom: Using re-enactment to enhance learning. *Social Education, 74,* 135–136.

Diener, E. (2000). Subjective well-being: The science of happiness and a proposal for a national index. *American Psychologist, 55,* 34–43. http://dx.doi.org/10.1037/0003-066X.55.1.34

Doman, G. J. (1966). *How to teach your child to read.* New York: Random House.

Downey, M., & Bliss, T. (2007). *Discover Colorado: Its people, places, and times.* Boulder: University Press of Colorado.

Draper, R. J., Broomhead, P., Jensen, A. P., Nokes, J. D., & Siebert, D. (Eds.). (2010). *(Re)Imagining content-area literacy instruction.* New York: Teachers College Press.

Dweck, C. (2006). *Mindset: The new psychology of success.* New York: Ballantine.

Echevarria, J., Short, D., & Vogt, M. E. (2011). *Making content comprehensible for English learners: The SIOP model.* Boston: Pearson Education.

Erekson, J. A., High, M. L., & Baldwin, S. (2005, February). *Acceleration vs. remediation: When one year's growth is not enough.* Paper presented at the Colorado Council of the International Reading Association, Denver, Colorado.

Farrington, C. A., Roderick, M., Allensworth, E., Nagaoka, J., Keyes, T. S., Johnson, D. W., & Beechum, N. O. (2012). *Teaching adolescents to become learners. The role of noncognitive factors in shaping school performance: A critical literature review.* Chicago: University of Chicago Consortium on Chicago School Research.

Filipovich, A. J., & Ozturk, T. (2012). Teaching the social studies through your local community. *Social Education, 76,* 85–87.

Flurkey, A. (2006). What's "normal" about real reading? In K. Goodman (Ed.), *The truth about DIBELS: What it is, what it does* (pp. 40–49). Portsmouth, NH: Heinemann.

Fry, S., Griffin, S., & Kirshner, J. (2012). Students and teachers in Belize and the U.S. take action together. *Social Studies and the Young Learner, 25*(21), 23–27.

Guccione, L. M. (2011). Integrating literacy and inquiry for English learners. *The Reading Teacher, 64,* 567–577.

Guthrie, J., & Wigfield, A. (1997). *Reading engagement: Motivating readers through integrated instruction.* Newark, DE: International Reading Association.

Hattie, J. (2012). Visible learning for teachers. *British Journal of Educational Technology, 43,* E134–E136). http://dx.doi.org/10.1111/j.1467-8535.2012.01347_7.x

International Reading Association. (2010). *Response to intervention: Guiding principles for educators.* Newark, DE: Author. Retrieved from http://www.reading.org/Libraries/resources /RTI_brochure_web.pdf

Johnston, P. H. (1997). *Knowing literacy: Constructive literacy assessment.* Portland, ME: Stenhouse.

Kopkowski, C. (2008, April). Why they leave. *NEA Today.* Retrieved from http://www.nea.org /home/12630.htm

Krashen, S. D. (1987). *Principles and practice in second language acquisition.* Englewood Cliffs, NJ: Prentice Hall.

Kucer, S. (2009). *Dimensions of literacy: A conceptual base for teaching reading and writing in school settings* (3rd ed.). Mahwah, NJ: Erlbaum.

Lakoff, G., & Johnson, M. (2003). *Metaphors we live by.* Chicago: University of Chicago Press.

Lee, J. K. (2004). Pre-service social studies teachers using digital civic resources. *International Journal of Social Education, 21,* 95–110.

Lewis, B. (1998). *The kid's guide to social action: How to solve the social problems you choose and turn creative thinking into positive action.* Minneapolis, MN: Free Spirit Press.

Lewis, B. A. (1989). The children's cleanup crusade. *Sierra, 74*(2), 62.

Loyd, S. M. (2011). *Beyond sentiment: A descriptive case study of elementary school teachers' experiences selecting children's literature for read-alouds.* (Doctoral dissertation.) Retrieved from UMI. (3493623)

McFadyen, J. (2012). A rain garden for our school: Becoming environmental stewards. *Social Studies and the Young Learner, 24*(3), 4–7.

Medina, J. (2008). *Brain rules: 12 principles for surviving and thriving at work, home, and school.* Seattle, WA: Pear Press.

Murdock, G. P. (1945). The common denominator of culture. In Linton, R. (Ed.). *The science of man in the world crisis.* New York: Columbia University Press.

National Council for the Social Studies. (2010). *National curriculum standards for social studies: A framework for teaching, learning, and assessment.* Silver Spring, MD: Author.

National Council for the Social Studies. (2013). *The college, career, and civic life (C3) framework for social studies state standards: Guidance for enhancing the rigor of K–12 civics, economics, geography, and history.* Silver Spring, MD: Author. Retrieved from http://www.socialstudies.org/C3

National Governors Association Center for Best Practices, Council of Chief State School Officers. (2010). *Common Core State Standards for English language arts and literacy in history/social studies, science, and technical subjects*. Washington, DC: Author. Retrieved from http://www.corestandards.org/

Olson, K. (2009). *Wounded by school: Recapturing the joy in learning and standing up to old school culture*. New York: Teachers College Press.

Opitz, M. F. (1998). *Flexible grouping in reading: Practical ways to help all students become better readers*. New York: Scholastic.

Opitz, M. F., & Ford, M. P. (2008). *Do-able differentiation: Varying groups, texts, and supports to reach readers*. Portsmouth, NH: Heinemann.

Opitz, M. F., & Ford, M. P. (2014). *Engaging minds in the classroom: The surprising power of joy*. Alexandria, VA: ASCD.

Opitz, M. F., Ford, M. P., & Erekson, J. A. (2011). *Accessible assessment: How 9 sensible techniques can power data-driven reading instruction*. Portsmouth, NH: Heinemann.

Pintrich, P. R., Marx, R. W., & Boyle, R. A. (1993). Beyond cold conceptual change: The role of motivational beliefs and classroom contextual factors in the process of conceptual change. *Review of Educational Research, 63*, 167–199. http://dx.doi.org/10.3102/00346543063002167

Rantala, T., & Maatta, K. (2012). Ten theses of the joy of learning at primary schools. *Early Child Development and Care, 182*(1), 87–105. http://dx.doi.org/10.1080/03004430.2010.545124

Ravitch, D. (2010). *The death and life of the great American school system: How testing and choice are undermining education*. New York: Basic Books.

Robinson, F. P. (1970). *Effective study* (4th ed.). New York: Harper & Row.

Rueda, R. (2011). *The 3 dimensions of improving student performance*. New York: Teachers College Press.

Sahlberg, P., & Hargreaves, A. (2011). *Finnish lessons: What the world can learn from educational change in Finland*. New York: Teachers College Press.

Schlechty, P. C. (2011). *Engaging students: The next level of working on the work*. San Francisco: Jossey-Bass.

Short, D. J. (1997). Reading and 'riting and . . . social studies: Research on integrated language and content in secondary classrooms. In M. A. Snow & D. M. Brinton (Eds.) *The content-based classroom* (pp. 213–232). White Plains, NY: Addison-Wesley/Longman.

Slauter, E. (2011, July 3). Life, liberty, and the pursuit of happiness. *Boston Globe.* Retrieved from http://www.boston.com/bostonglobe/ideas/articles/2011/07/03/life_liberty_and_the_pursuit_of_happiness/

Stanovich, K. (1986). Matthew effects in reading: Some consequences of individual differences in the acquisition of literacy. *Reading Research Quarterly, 21*, 360–404. Retrieved from http://www.psychologytoday.com/files/u81/Stanovich__1986_.pdf

Stodolsky, S. S., Salk, S., & Glaessner, B. (1991). Student views about learning math and social studies. *American Educational Research Journal, 28*, 89–116. http://dx.doi.org/10.3102/00028312028001089

Stone, A. A., Schwartz, J. E., Broderick, J. E., & Deaton, A. (2010). A snapshot of the age distribution of psychological well-being in the United States. *Proceedings of the National Academy of Sciences of the United States of America, 107*, 9985–9990. http://dx.doi.org/10.1073/pnas.1003744107

Taylor, B. M., Pearson, P. D., Clark, K., & Walpole, S. (2000). Effective schools and accomplished teachers: Lessons about primary-grade reading instruction in low-income schools. *Elementary School Journal, 101*, 121–165. http://dx.doi.org/10.1086/499662

Thompson, S. (1966). *Motif index of folk literature*. Bloomington: Indiana University Press.

Thompson, S. C., & Williams, K. N. (2008). *Telling stories with photo essays: A guide for preK–5 teachers*. Thousand Oaks, CA: Corwin.

Todorov, K. R., & Brousseau, B. (1998). *Authentic assessment of social studies*. Lansing, MI: Michigan Department of Education.

Tough, P. (2012). *How children succeed: Grit, curiosity, and the hidden power of character*. Boston: Houghton Mifflin.

Vygotsky, L. S. (1978). *Mind in society: The development of higher psychological processes*. Cambridge, MA: Harvard University Press.

Vygotsky, L. S. (1986). *Thought and language* (Rev. ed.). Cambridge, MA: MIT Press.

Ward, G., & Dahlmeier, C. (2011). Rediscovering joyfulness. *Young Children, 66*(6), 94–98.

Wasicsko, M. (2007). The perceptual approach to teacher dispositions: The effective teacher as an effective person. In M. E. Diez & J. D. Raths (Eds.), *Teacher dispositions: Their nature, development and assessment*. Charlotte, NC: Information Age Publishing.

Wolk, S. (2008). Joyful learning can flourish in school if you give joy a chance. *Educational Leadership, 66*(1), 8–15.

Wright, S. P., Horn, S. P., & Sanders, W. L. (1997). Teacher and classroom context effects on student achievement: Implications for teacher evaluation. *Journal of Personnel Evaluation in Education, 11*, 57–67.

Zhao, Y. (2009). *Catching up or leading the way? American education in the age of globalization*. Alexandria, VA: ASCD.

Index

Note: The letter *f* following a page number denotes a figure.

accountability, joyful learning's support for, 48–49

achievement, mindset-performance correlation, 3–4

achievement gaps, joyful learning to address, 44–46

anxiety, evaluating in learners, 15*f*

Archaeology Dig Box (activity), 34*f*

assessment. *See also* standards
in the joyful learning framework, 12, 12*f*
joyful learning's support for, 48–49
of learners, 13–14, 15*f*
of schoolwide configurations, 21
self-reporting used in, 10–11
in social studies, principles of, 20
teacher self-assessment, 14–17, 16*f*
of texts and materials, 17–19

attributions, description and instructional implications, 7*f*

authentic texts, assessing, 18–19

autonomy, engagement and, 9–10

brain, thinking and feeling areas of the, 1

C3 framework, 46–47

challenge, evaluating learner's perceptions, 15*f*

choice, incorporating, 9–10

Circular Flow Simulation (activity), 34*f*

civic competence
modeling in the classroom, 27–28
social action projects, 24–27, 27*f*

classroom environment
long-term inquiry learning, 28–30, 29*f*
modeling civic competence, 27–28
social systems, creating, 30–31

classroom materials, assessing, 17–19

cognitive memory, 1–2

collaboration, teacher self-assessment of, 16*f*

Common Core State Standards (CCSS)
for K-12 social studies, 19–20

competence beliefs
description and instructional implications, 7*f*
small-group instruction, 35

concrete concepts activities, 32–33, 34*f*

control beliefs, description and instructional implications, 7*f*

Council of Chief State School Officers (CCSS), 46–47

critical thinking skills development, 36–37, 38*f*

curiosity, evaluating in learners, 15*f*

engagement
autonomy and, 9–10
choice and, 9–10
education vs., 6, 8
modeling, 17, 19
motivation vs., 6, 8
in social studies, 8–9
teacher self-assessment of, 16*f*, 17

feedback use, teacher self-assessment, 16*f*

goal orientation
evaluating in learners, 15*f*
instructional implications of, 7*f*

identity
  evaluating in learners,
    15f
  teacher self-assessment
    of, 15–16
individual instruction
  opportunities of, 37, 39
  universal experiences,
    40–41, 41f
  visual essays, 39–40
inquiry learning, 28–30, 29f
instruction, open sourcing,
  17

joyful learning
  accountability, support
    for, 48–49
  achievement gaps,
    addressing, 44–46
  assessment, support for,
    48–49
  foundational skills, 5
  goal of, 4
  implementation within
    RTI frameworks,
    43–44, 45f
  modeling, 17
  in social studies, 5–6, 19
  standards, correlation to,
    46–48
joyful learning framework
  assessment and
    evaluation
    components, 12, 12f
  learning environments
    and configurations for,
    12, 12f, 23
  motivational
    generalizations, 7f,
    11, 12f
  overview, 12f

learners
  achievement gaps, joyful
    learning to address,
    44–46
  evaluating, 13–14, 15f
learning, rewards
  encouraging, 5–6

learning environments in the
  joyful learning framework,
  12, 12f
Living History (activity), 34f

manipulatives, assessing, 18
Matthew Effect, 44
Metronome Steps (activity),
  34f
motivation
  engagement vs., 6, 8
  factors influencing, 6
  Matthew Effect of,
    44–45
motivational generalizations
  instructional
    implications, 7f
  in the joyful learning
    framework, 11, 12f

National Council for the
  Social Studies, 5, 24
National Curriculum
  Standards for Social
  Studies (NCSS), 46
noncognitive skills, 1–4

Opportunity Cost (activity),
  34f

performance-mindset
  correlation, 3–4
persistence, evaluating in
  learners, 15f
prosocial behaviors,
  evaluating in learners, 15f

questions, exploring with,
  40

Response to Intervention
  (RTI), 43–44, 45f

school community social
  action projects, 24–27, 27f
schoolwide configurations,
  assessment of, 21
self-assessment, modeling,
  10

self-efficacy, learner
  description and
    instructional
    implications, 7f
  evaluating, 15f
  small-group instruction
    and, 35
self-regulating behaviors,
  evaluating in learners, 15f
self-reporting, 10–11
small-group instruction
  critical thinking skills
    development, 36–37,
    38f
  on learning to read social
    studies texts, 33, 35,
    36f
social action projects, 24–27,
  27f
social developmental theory,
  10
social studies
  attitudes toward, factors
    in, 11
  CCSS standards for K-12,
    19–20
  defined, 24
  goal of, 5
  joyful learning in, 5–6,
    19
  principles of assessment
    in, 20
social studies texts
  assessing, 17–19
  learning to read, 33, 35,
    36f
social systems, creating in
  the classroom, 30–31
standards. See also
  assessment
  CCSS for K-12 social
    studies, 19–20
  joyful learning's
    correlation to, 46–48

teachers
  effective, traits of, 14
  engagement, modeling,
    17

teachers *(continued)*
  motivation, modeling, 35
  self-advocacy, 48
  self-assessments, 14–17,
    16f
tests, 19–20. *See also*
  assessment
textbooks
  assessing, 17–19
  learning to read, 33, 35,
    36f
Thinking Like an Expert
  (small-group activity), 38f
Time Change (activity), 34f

transparency, teaching and
  learning, 17
Traveling Trunk (activity), 34f

universal experiences,
  40–41, 41f

valuing
  evaluating in learners, 15f
  instructional implications
    of, 7f
visual essays, 39–40
visual experiences activities,
  31–32

Walk through History
  (activity), 34f
Whale to Scale (activity), 34f
What Is the Human
  Experience? (individual
  activity), 41f
whole-group instruction
  concrete concepts
    activities in, 32–33,
    34f
  visual experiences
    activities in, 31–32

About the Author

James A. Erekson is an associate professor of reading at the University of Northern Colorado. He has been teaching in the field of languages and literacy for more than 20 years, teaching four foreign languages in addition to reading and language arts courses. Erekson collaborates with K–12 educators to teach and do research on reading, writing, and oral language. He taught elementary grades and collaborated with middle school teachers to coordinate a successful reading center for eight years, where the vitality of social studies content helped young readers make breakthroughs in reading and writing. Erekson has presented his work both nationally and internationally, and he recently worked with Denver Public Schools' elementary teachers on a three-year state-funded learning experience on social studies and literacy.

About the Editors

Michael F. Opitz is professor emeritus of reading education at the University of Northern Colorado, where he taught undergraduate and graduate courses. An author and literacy consultant, Michael provides inservice and staff development sessions and presents at state and international conferences and also works with elementary school teachers to plan, teach, and evaluate lessons focused on different aspects of literacy. He is the author and coauthor of numerous books, articles, and reading programs.

Michael P. Ford is chair of and professor in the Department of Literacy and Language at the University of Wisconsin Oshkosh, where he teaches undergraduate and graduate courses. He is a former Title I reading and 1st grade teacher. Michael is the author of 5 books and more than 30 articles. Michael has worked with teachers throughout the country and his work with the international school network has included staff development presentations in the Middle East, Europe, Africa, South America, and Central America.

Friends and colleagues for more than two decades, Opitz and Ford began working together as a result of their common reading education interests. Through their publications and presentations, they continue to help educators reach readers through thoughtful, purposeful instruction grounded in practical theory.

Related ASCD Resources:
Engaging and Joyful Teaching and Learning in Social Studies

At the time of publication, the following ASCD resources were available (ASCD stock numbers appear in parentheses). For up-to-date information about ASCD resources, go to www.ascd.org.

ASCD EDge Group
Exchange ideas and connect with other educators interested in differentiated instruction on the social networking site ASCD EDge™ at http://ascdedge.ascd.org.

Print Products
Building Learning Communities with Character: How to Integrate Academic, Social, and Emotional Learning Bernard Novick, Jeffrey S. Kress, and Maurice J. Elias (#101240)

Closing the Attitude Gap: How to Fire Up Your Students to Strive for Success Baruti K. Kafele (#114006)

Create Success!: Unlocking the Potential of Urban Students Kadhir Rajagopal (#111022)

Creating the Opportunity to Learn: Moving from Research to Practice to Close the Achievement Gap A. Wade Boykin and Pedro Noguera (#197157)

Curriculum 21: Essential Education for a Changing World edited by Heidi Hayes Jacobs (#109008)

Developing Habits of Mind in Elementary Schools: An ASCD Action Tool Karen Boyes and Graham Watts (#108015)

Developing Habits of Mind in Secondary Schools: An ASCD Action Tool Karen Boyes and Graham Watts (#109108)

Engaging the Whole Child: Reflections on Best Practices in Learning, Teaching, and Leadership edited by Marge Scherer and the Educational Leadership Staff (#109103)

Everyday Engagement: Making Students and Parents Your Partners in Learning Katy Ridnouer (#109009)

Flip Your Classroom: Reach Every Student in Every Class Every Day Jonathan Bergmann and Aaron Sams (#112060)

The Formative Assessment Action Plan: Practical Steps to More Successful Teaching and Learning Nancy Frey and Douglas Fisher (#111013)

Habits of Mind Across the Curriculum: Practical and Creative Strategies for Teachers edited by Arthur L. Costa and Bena Kallick (#108014)

How to Create a Culture of Achievement in Your School and Classroom Douglas Fisher, Nancy Frey, and Ian Pumpian (#111014)

How to Motivate Reluctant Learners Robyn R. Jackson (#110076)

Learning and Leading with Habits of Mind: 16 Essential Characteristics for Success edited by Arthur L. Costa and Bena Kallick (#108008)

Managing Diverse Classrooms: How to Build on Students' Cultural Strengths Carrie Rothstein-Fisch and Elise Trumbull (#107014)

Priorities in Practice: The Essentials of Social Studies, Grades K–8: Effective Curriculum, Instruction, and Assessment Kathy Checkley (#107099)

Promoting Social and Emotional Learning: Guidelines for Educators Maurice J. Elias, Joseph E. Zins, Roger P. Weissberg, Karin S. Frey, Mark T. Greenberg, Norris M. Haynes, Rachael Kessler, Mary E. Schwab-Stone, and Timothy P. Shriver (#197157)

Teaching English Language Learners Across the Content Areas Judie Haynes and Debbie Zacarian (#109032)

Teaching Every Student in the Digital Age: Universal Design for Learning David H. Rose, Anne Meyer, Nicole Strangman, and Gabrielle Rappolt (#101042)

Totally Positive Teaching: A Five-Stage Approach to Energizing Students and Teachers Joseph Ciaccio (#104016)

Transformational Teaching in the Information Age: Making Why and How We Teach Relevant to Students Thomas R. Rosebrough and Ralph G. Leverett (#110078)

The Whole Child Initiative helps schools and communities create learning environments that allow students to be healthy, safe, engaged, supported, and challenged. To learn more about other books and resources that relate to the whole child, visit www.wholechildeducation.org.

For more information: send e-mail to member@ascd.org; call 1-800-933-2723 or 703-578-9600, press 2; send a fax to 703-575-5400; or write to Information Services, ASCD, 1703 N. Beauregard St., Alexandria, VA 22311-1714 USA.